BELMONT

THE RIDGEWAY, MILL HILL

ET VIRTUTEM ET MUSAS

LIBRARY & MEDIA
RESOURCE CENTRE

Telephone 020 8959 1431

What if we do
nOthing?

WATER SUPPLY

Rob Bowden

W
FRANKLIN WATTS
LONDON • SYDNEY

First published in 2006 by Franklin Watts
Reprinted 2007

Copyright © 2006 Arcturus Publishing Limited

Franklin Watts
338 Euston Road
London NW1 3BH

Franklin Watts Australia
Hachette Children's Books
Level 17/207 Kent St, Sydney, NSW 2000

Produced by Arcturus Publishing Limited,
26/27 Bickels Yard, 151-153 Bermondsey Street, London SE1 3HA

Series concept: Alex Woolf
Editor: Alex Woolf
Designer: Peta Morey
Picture researcher: Glass Onion Pictures
Consultant: Professor Mike Edmunds

Picture Credits
Corbis: 32 (Caroline Penn), 34 (Faisal Mahmood/Reuters).
NASA: 4 (Reto Stöckli/Robert Simmon/MODIS/USGS/Defense Meteorological Program).
Rex Features: 8 (Wildtrack Media), 11 (Sipa Press), 14 (Sipa Press), 16 (Sipa Press), 28
(Phil Ball), 36 (N. Bostram/IBL).
Still Pictures: 7 (Nutta Yooyean/UNEP), 13 (Gil Moti), 18 (Mark Edwards), 21 (Joerg
Boethling), 23 (Mark Shenley), 25 (B. Blume/UNEP), 27 (Gil Moti), 30 (Mark Edwards),
38 (Jorgen Schytte), 40 (Jorgen Schytte), 42 (Ron Giling/Lineair), 44 (Bojan Brecelj).

A CIP catalogue record for this book is available from the British Library

Dewey Decimal Classification Number: 363.6'1

ISBN 978 0 7496 6616 3

Printed in China

Franklin Watts is a division of Hachette Childen's Books

Contents

CHAPTER 1

Water Crisis

It is May 2020 and world leaders are gathered in Shanghai, China, for a vital international summit. Their agenda for discussion includes a major war, the annual death of millions of innocent people and the sickness suffered by hundreds of millions of others. This is not a discussion following the outbreak of nuclear war or the aftermath of a biological terrorist attack. They are discussing water.

Back in the 1990s scientists and environmentalists had begun to warn political leaders about a potential water crisis in the early 21st century, but they were too slow to take action. There have now been several wars over access to water, including a major conflict between Ethiopia and Egypt over the use of the Nile's waters. Over a billion people suffer regular ill health due to a lack of clean water and access to sanitation, and an estimated four billion (over half the world total) live in countries where water resources are stressed or scarce (see table on page 5). As world leaders search for a solution, too many people still take water for granted.

Thankfully, this meeting has not yet happened, but the warnings and some of the outcomes are very real. Many water experts believe that water supplies are at, or fast approaching, crisis point. If we do nothing then the above scenario could easily happen, and what is more, it could be much, much worse.

The importance of water

Water is vital for virtually all life on Earth. As humans we can go many days without food, but without water we would perish in just 48 hours. In fact in some very harsh conditions, such as extreme heat, we may only have a few hours' survival time. So why is water so important? Well, it makes up around 70 percent of the human body and so without it our bodies simply fail. Most other living things on our planet also comprise a high proportion of water and so are equally dependent. There are plants and animals that have been able to adapt to extremely dry conditions such as those found in desert regions, but ultimately they all require some water in order to survive.

A world of water

Unless you live in the middle of a desert, you could be forgiven for wondering why we need to worry about water. After all, it appears to be everywhere. It falls as rain; our rivers and lakes are full of it; the seas and oceans have water as far as the eye can see; and we only need turn on a tap to get a non-stop supply right in our homes.

When viewed from space it is easy to see that our planet is dominated by water. In fact water covers around 71 percent of the Earth, but despite this there are parts of the world where people have barely enough to survive.

LEVELS OF WATER CRISIS

These are the four main levels used to discuss the world water crisis:

Cubic metres of water per person per year	Classification
1700-2000	Water shortages
1000-1699	Water stress
500-999	Water scarcity
0-499	Absolute water scarcity

Source: Sustaining Water, Population Action International

In some respects you would be right because water makes up 70.7 percent of the total surface area of our planet, a total of 360 million square kilometres. Not only does it cover a vast area, but of course water can also be very deep. Lake Baikal in Russia, for example, is over 1.6 kilometres deep, and the Pacific, Atlantic and Indian Oceans have an average depth of between 3.7 and 4.3 kilometres. The volume of water on our planet is therefore even more impressive, at an estimated 1.338 billion cubic kilometres. This is hard to imagine, but just one cubic kilometre is the equivalent of a thousand billion litres of water, which if you drank the recommended five litres of water a day would last you for over 547 million years!

The problem with water

Unfortunately not all of the water on Earth is available for human use. To begin with, most of it (97.5 percent) is salt water, found in the world's seas and oceans. Humans are unable to drink salt water without expensive desalination treatment (see page 13) and very few crops can tolerate salt water. This leaves just 2.5 percent of water as

THE WORLD'S WATER

Salt water	% of total water
Oceans/seas	96.54
Saline/brackish groundwater	0.93
Saltwater lakes	0.006
Fresh water	
Glaciers, permanent snowcover	1.74
Fresh groundwater	0.76
Ground ice, permafrost	0.022
Freshwater lakes	0.007
Soil moisture	0.001
Atmospheric water vapour	0.001
Marshes, wetlands	0.001
Rivers	0.0002
Incorporated in living things	0.0001

Source: Sustaining Water, Population Action International

fresh water and of this most is tied up in glaciers, snow and ice fields, or deep groundwater reserves. The water we use for drinking and bathing, for growing food, and for industry comes from rainwater, rivers, lakes, soil moisture and shallow groundwater reservoirs. These sources make up less than one percent of the world's fresh water supply, or less than 0.02 percent of the planet's total water.

A renewable resource

Thankfully, water is a renewable resource that is constantly recycled and replaced as part of the global hydrological cycle. The time taken to renew supplies can be quite rapid, such as when a reservoir fills up following a period of heavy rainfall. Other supplies are renewed at a much slower rate, however. Some groundwater supplies (water stored within the rocks underground) can take thousands of years to be replenished by the very gradual infiltration of water. When considering water use it is therefore important to think about the sustainability of supplies and their renewal rates.

Who has the water?

In addition to there being relatively little water available for human use, it is also very unevenly distributed. Countries such as Brazil and Canada have an abundance of water, whereas others like Israel and Spain can sometimes struggle to meet even their basic needs. There are also enormous inequalities within countries. In a large country like China, for instance, some areas suffer regular flooding whilst others struggle with the permanent threat of drought.

Villagers rest on the dried bed of a local water source in Konkean Province, Thailand. Many water sources around the world are drying up rapidly.

WORLD'S FRESH WATER DISTRIBUTION	
Brazil	17%
Russia	11%
Canada	7%
China	7%
Indonesia	6%
USA	6%
Bangladesh	6%
India	5%
Other	35%

Source: World Commission on Dams, 2000

AVERAGE ANNUAL WATER SUPPLY PER PERSON, BY CONTINENT	
Continent	**Cubic metres**
Africa	5,720
Asia	3,920
Australia and Oceania	82,200
Europe	4,230
North & Central America	17,400
South America	38,200

Source: The World's Water, 2000-2001

At a global level, Asia, South America and North and Central America are the continents with the highest amount of available water. Africa, Europe and Australia and Oceania have the least available. Asia has almost five times the water availability of Europe and six times that of Australia and Oceania.

The global availability changes, however, if population is taken into account and we think about the amount of water available per person at a given location. Asia, for example, despite having the highest total available water supply, has the least of all the continents when considered per person because of its enormous population. In contrast, the very low population of Australia and Oceania means it has the highest amount of water per person, despite having the lowest total availability.

A crisis in the making

At the start of the 21st century, many parts of the world are facing serious water shortages. In 2000, 49 countries (including India, Kenya, Nigeria and

An ox is used to draw water from a well in India. Of all the continents, Asia has the least amount of water per person.

Ethiopia) had annual renewable fresh water availability of less than 2,000 cubic metres – the level below which countries are considered chronically short. Population growth is a key factor in this, but not the only one. Our diets and lifestyles also have a major impact. To produce one kilogram of potatoes, for example, requires up to 1,500 kilograms of water (one kilogram of water is equal to one litre), but to produce one kilogram of beef requires up to 70,000 kilograms of water. If the trend towards more meat-based diets continues then it will clearly have a considerable impact on water use.

Water supplies are already problematic in many countries, and water shortages affect around a third of the world's population. Yet the use of water by humans is expected to increase by a further 30 percent by 2025. This worries many scientists who believe that if we do nothing the 21st century could see environmental disasters, human tragedies and even war – all as a result of water. This book will examine some of those concerns and consider what the solutions might be.

DEBATE

You are in charge
You are a government minister who has to address a regional conference on how to avoid a future water crisis in your country and region. Some initial ideas have been suggested:

- Invest money in searching for new sources of water to increase supplies.
- Develop pipelines to transfer water from regions of plenty to those where water is scarce.
- Launch an education programme to change people's lifestyles and reduce water use in the first place.
- Introduce high water pricing to make people realize the value of water and treat it as a scarce resource.

What will you make your priority? Do you have any additional suggestions for avoiding a future water crisis?

CHAPTER 2

The Quest for Water

The year is 2025, and a ceremony has been held in Khartoum, Sudan, to mark the completion of the Highlands Pipeline. This ambitious project will bring water from the Ethiopian highlands via a giant pipeline to the people of Ethiopia and Sudan. It has taken engineers seven years to build the pipeline across mountainous terrain at a cost of billions of dollars. It is hoped that the water, which will begin flowing later this year, will bring an end to the droughts and famines that have plagued this part of Africa since the 1970s. A Sudanese minister said, '2025 will be remembered as a year of great triumph, a year in which we finally conquered nature to bring guaranteed water to our people and end hunger in our country forever'.

This might sound like an impossible dream, but at the start of the 21st century the quest for more secure water supplies has led several countries to invest in such projects. Libya, for example, began building its Great Man-Made River in 1984 to extract water from aquifers (underground stores of water) deep under the Sahara Desert.

Pipelines under the desert

Libya, much of which comprises desert, has very little available fresh water, but in the 1950s, during a search for oil in the Sahara, enormous aquifers were discovered. These contain water that may have been there for up to 100,000 years. Giant pipelines have been constructed to carry this water under the desert to the main population and agricultural areas along the Mediterranean coast. At four metres in diameter and over 1,600 kilometres long, the pipelines carry around 6.5 million cubic metres per day. The project is still expanding and will not be complete until 2025, by which time Colonel Qaddafi, the Libyan leader, says the water will make Libya's deserts as green as its flag.

Digging deep

Libya's Great Man-Made River is the biggest engineering project in the world and an example of the extremes that countries will go to in order to secure water supplies. Libya is not alone in adopting such measures, and billions of dollars are spent every year across the globe in order to increase water supplies. One of the most common ways to do this is to drill for groundwater stored in aquifers. Many of the world's largest cities, including Mexico City, London and Jakarta, are dependent on aquifers to meet most, or all, of their water needs.

This giant section of pipeline is just part of Libya's Great Man-Made River project.

THE IMPORTANCE OF AQUIFERS

Aquifers:
- hold approximately 97 percent of the world's liquid fresh water
- contain water that has been there for an average of 1,400 years
- are the main source of drinking water for up to two billion people
- provide 99 percent of the rural population in the United States with drinking water
- account for over 50 percent of India's irrigation water and 40 percent of agricultural output
- supply Europe with 75 percent of its total drinking water

Source: Worldwatch Institute, 2001

Rural areas, too remote to be connected to piped water systems, are heavily dependent on dug wells and small boreholes (sometimes known as tube wells) drilled to access underground water supplies. During the 1980s, millions of boreholes were drilled across the world as part of the United Nations International Decade for Water. By the mid-1990s India alone had over six million boreholes, compared to just 3,000 in 1950. In neighbouring Bangladesh, over 95 percent of the population relies on boreholes for drinking water.

Aquifers can provide a quick and relatively cheap solution to water shortages, but experience around the world has highlighted several problems. These include groundwater pollution, excessive extraction, subsidence and saltwater contamination. (These problems will be covered in more detail in Chapter 3.) Nevertheless, until other solutions are found, aquifers remain the best source of water for up to a third of the world's people.

Harvesting water

People have harvested water for centuries using a variety of methods. If you have a garden you may even do it yourself, using a water butt to collect rainwater for watering the plants. In the face of shortages, water harvesting is now becoming a serious option for improving supplies. In Tokyo, Japan, for example, the large public forecourt of the metropolitan government offices is built at a gradient to gather rainfall that is then used for flushing toilets.

Water harvesting can also take place on a much larger scale, as in the fishing village of Chungungo in northern Chile. Chungungo relied on water being trucked in to meet its needs until, in 1987, a fog-harvesting scheme was built on the ridge above the village. Seventy-five giant mesh screens were strung between posts to catch the sea fogs that rolled in over the village every morning. As the fog hits the mesh it forms droplets that fall to the bottom of the screen to be carried away in collectors for storage. The residents of

LESSONS FROM NATURE

The Namib fog beetle (*Onymacris unguicularis*) climbs each morning to the top of a sand dune in the Namib Desert of southern Africa. Once there it turns into the wind and tips its body into the breeze. The fog that rolls in from the sea each morning condenses on the beetle's back and rolls down its body to reach its mouth, providing a refreshing drink in an environment that has virtually no fresh water. This brilliant method of collecting water is the inspiration for today's fog-harvesting schemes.

Chungungo now have a daily supply of around 40 litres of water each from the fog-harvesters, and there is even a surplus to allow the cultivation of crops and trees.

The success of fog-harvesting in Chungungo has been copied elsewhere in Chile as well as in Peru, Oman and South Africa. Other countries and areas with regular foggy conditions could also benefit from this cheap, simple and sustainable way of securing water.

These fog-harvesting screens in Chungungo, Chile, have been used to provide the village with fresh water since 1987.

Desalination

For countries with limited sources of fresh water, but access to seawater or other saline (salt-containing) water, a process called desalination can be used to remove salt to create fresh water. Desalination is widely used in the Middle East, North Africa and by various island communities, some of which are entirely dependent on desalination.

Desalination would seem to be an ideal solution to the problem of water supply because the oceans offer an endless and continually renewed supply of water. The process of desalination is expensive, however, and produces water at several times the cost of other methods. The process also requires a lot of energy and so can have negative environmental effects unless the energy used is from renewable sources. At the beginning of the 21st century there are around 120 countries with desalination plants, but their combined annual output is only about as much water as the world's population would use in 14 hours.

Desalination, therefore, does not offer a global solution, but is very important to countries with minimal fresh water and where alternatives may not be available. In the future, if we fail to conserve current supplies, then desalination could become a key technology.

industrial products
10%

livestock and livestock products
23%

crops and cereals
67%

Water is traded around the world in the form of products that use water in their creation. This chart shows how the world's water trade is divided by product type.

Source: International Year of Freshwater, 2003

A desalination plant at Dhahran, Saudi Arabia. With almost no fresh water supplies of its own, Saudi Arabia is a world leader in desalination technology.

Trading water

Some countries have turned to purchasing water to meet their needs. Turkey, for example, sells water to Israel and Cyprus. The water is towed across the Mediterranean in giant plastic bags. Turkey also has plans for pipelines and supertankers to deliver water to other water-scarce neighbours. Tankers already deliver water from other countries to islands in the Bahamas and to Japan, Korea and Taiwan, and there are plans for more pipelines and tankers to further increase the global trade in water.

There is also a trade in 'virtual water' – the water used to produce crops and livestock (and industrial goods) that are then exported. This virtual water is thought to account for around 15 percent of the world's current water use. A single tonne of wheat, for example, uses around 1,000 tonnes of water, and so for a country facing water shortages it is easier to import grain than it is to import the water to grow it.

Water-stressed nations already import a quarter of the world's grain, and as more nations become water-stressed they are likely to add to this trade in virtual water. Some of those nations, such as China and India, are currently exporters of grain and so there is concern as to whether there will be enough grain to go around should water shortages force them to become importers too.

DEBATE

You are in charge
You work for a major private water company that is looking to increase its supplies due to growing demand. The following three options are available:

1. Build a desalination plant to provide fresh water into the existing system.
2. Construct a pipeline to buy and transport water from your neighbouring country that has a plentiful supply of water.
3. Drill deep boreholes to explore for fossil groundwater (water stored from prehistoric times when the climate was wetter) contained in aquifers.

What will you make your priority? Do you have any additional suggestions for avoiding a future water crisis?

CHAPTER 3

Messing with Nature

Nataliya sits on the balcony of her house in Uzbekistan with her granddaughter Mina, who has come to visit. They stare out at the desert in front of them and Mina asks what the large, angular shapes are on the horizon. 'Why don't you get your grandfather's binoculars and have a look,' replies Nataliya. Mina looks through the heavy binoculars and to her amazement she sees several large fishing boats. 'What are they doing in the middle of the desert?' she asks. Nataliya explains that when she was a little girl in the 1950s the land in front of them was all water, part of the world's fourth-biggest lake, the Aral Sea. It once had a busy fishing industry, but then the waters feeding the lake were diverted for irrigating cotton and the lake began to shrink. Fishing boats were left stranded and by 2005 the shoreline had receded by up to 250 kilometres. 'Twenty years later and the lake has still not returned, despite efforts to undo the damage we have caused,' says Nataliya with a sad look in her eyes.

Warnings for tomorrow

The story of the Aral Sea is one of the great warnings to us all about the dangers of messing with nature. It is not the only one. In our continual search for water we have caused rivers to run dry, flooded entire communities, caused aquifers to sink, poisoned soils and destroyed habitats and wildlife.

The global demand for water for human use is expected to increase by at least 40 percent by the year 2025 and an estimated 17 percent more water will be needed to meet food needs, so it is

A fishing boat lies stranded far from the water in the barren landscape that was once the Aral Sea in Uzbekistan.

important that ways are found to work with nature and not against it. If we do nothing, then the disaster of the Aral Sea could be repeated across the world.

Diverting water

The shrinking of the Aral Sea has been caused by the diversion of water from the rivers that feed it. Diversion of water from rivers does not always cause problems, but when it disturbs natural processes the effects can often be devastating. The Huang He (Yellow River) in China, for example, has failed to reach the sea at certain times of the year (this happened for over 200 days in 1997) because of too much extraction of its waters further upstream. The Colorado River in the USA and the River Nile in Egypt have also failed to reach the sea in recent years.

SHRINKING LAKES

Excessive water use has caused around half of the world's lakes to suffer shrinkage or to disappear completely. Here are some examples.

Lake	Effect of water extraction
Lake Chad West Africa	Area reduced by 95% since 1960 due to increased extraction from the rivers feeding it, and droughts.
Aral Sea Kazakhstan/Uzbekistan	Area reduced by 80% since 1960; could disappear completely by 2020.
Dead Sea Israel/Jordan/Palestine	Extraction for irrigation is causing water levels to fall by up to a metre per year; could disappear by 2050.
Huang He Basin China	Since the 1980s about 3,000 of the 5,100 lakes along the course of the Huang He have disappeared.
Lake Chapala Mexico	Since the 1970s the lake has lost more than 80% of its water, due to irrigation and urban demand.
Owens Lake California, USA	Dried up completely in 1920s as water from Owens River was diverted to Los Angeles. The dried lake bed is USA's major source of particulate air pollution.
Dal Lake India	Lake has shrunk by half since 1980s and water levels by 2.4 metres in the period 1995-2005.

Source: Eco-Economy Updates, April 2005, Earth Policy Institute

When rivers fail to reach the sea, salt water can flow inland, destroying local habitats and wildlife that are unable to cope with the high salt levels. There is also a greater rate of coastal erosion as sand and silt that were once deposited by the river no longer provide protection from waves. Rivers also deliver high quantities of nutrients into the oceans, and fish stocks that rely on these for food can collapse if the rivers no longer reach the sea. This happened to sardine stocks in the eastern Mediterranean following the completion of the Aswan High Dam in Egypt. The dam stemmed the flow of nutrients from the River Nile and the annual sardine catch fell from 18,000 tonnes to just 500 tonnes.

Dams

People have been building dams for centuries as a way of capturing water for human use. In fact some of the earliest evidence of dam construction in Egypt and Jordan dates back over 5,000 years. Dams allow water to be stored, to be diverted (for irrigation or via pipelines to urban areas), and to generate electricity (a process known as hydro-electric power, or HEP). Dams are also built to protect people from the dangers of flooding, or to improve navigation. In the past,

Many of the world's rivers have been dammed to store their water for human use. This water reservoir is in Yorkshire in the UK and is very small. Some reservoirs stretch for hundreds of kilometres.

dams were relatively small and had only a minimal impact on natural environments.

At the start of the 20th century there were only a few hundred large dams (those over 15 metres in height) in existence. During the 20th century, however, dams became bigger and more widespread, thanks to advances in engineering. Some of the largest dams are now more than a kilometre wide and over 150 metres high. Globally, the number of large dams mushroomed from around 5,000 in 1950 to more than 45,000 in over 140 countries in 2005. China alone has some 22,000 large dams, compared to only 22 in 1949. The construction of large dams peaked in the 1970s and has now slowed considerably, but the World Commission on Dams reports that up to 300 large dams are still completed every year.

Large dams regulate almost half of the world's major water systems. They store roughly the equivalent of all water withdrawn for human use in a year. This massive disruption to the natural water cycle causes many problems. Up to 40 percent of water stored in dams may be lost by evaporation.

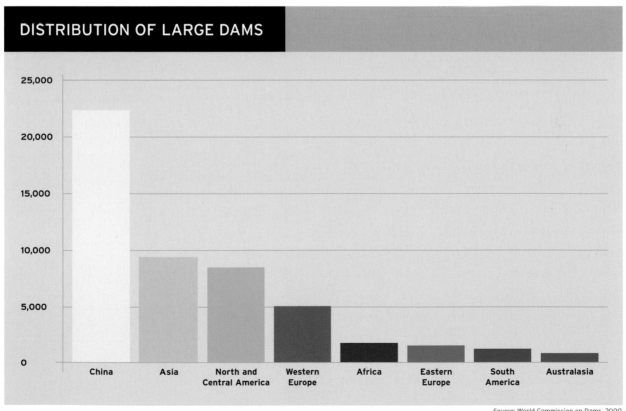

DISTRIBUTION OF LARGE DAMS

Source: World Commission on Dams, 2000.

We have already learnt that some rivers no longer reach the sea and about the problems of nutrients and sediments being trapped. Globally around 0.5 to 1 percent of storage capacity is lost every year because of sediment build-up behind dams. If this trend continues, by 2025 almost a quarter of the world's freshwater storage could be lost, at a time when population and demand will be even greater.

Large dams disrupt fish stocks and have played a part in the extinction of around 20 percent of the world's 9,000 freshwater fish species. The reservoirs created by large dams can also mean that whole communities have to be moved, and in total it is thought that 80 million people may have been displaced in recent decades because of dam construction. The exact numbers are hard to calculate because many of the people displaced live in countries with less developed economies where accurate records are not always available. In India, for example, the estimated number of people displaced by large dams ranges from 16 to 38 million.

Some experts claim that large dams have also caused an increased incidence of earthquakes in some areas and that the combined effect of water stored in their reservoirs has even caused a very slight wobble in the revolution of the Earth!

Irrigation

One of the primary reasons for building large dams is to provide water for irrigating farmland. Much of the water extracted from aquifers is also used for irrigation and, in total, farming accounts for around 70 percent of human water use. The area of farmland under irrigation increased more than fivefold during the 20th century and today covers between 250 and 275 million hectares. This is only about 17 percent of total farmland, but it accounts for around 40 percent of the world's total food production.

Irrigation is not all good news, however. In most irrigation systems there is a very high degree of wastage, with water lying on the surface or sinking into the ground rather than being used by the plants. The excessive use of water not only reduces supplies for

WORLD IRRIGATED AREA 1961-2002

Year	Million hectares
1961	139.1
1965	150.2
1970	168.0
1975	188.6
1980	210.2
1985	225.7
1990	245.0
1995	262.3
2000	275.2
2002	276.8

Source: UN Food and Agricultural Organization, 2005

alternative uses but can also lead to a damaging environmental problem called salinization. This happens when too much water is applied to crops. The water then evaporates and leaves behind high concentrations of mineral salts. Salts can also rise to the surface from shallow water tables and when the over-application of water causes the water table to rise.

A temple in Manibeli village in India lies submerged beneath the waters that have risen behind the Sardar Sarovar dam on the Narmada River.

When soils become too salty they are unfit for growing crops and productive farmland can be ruined. Across the world around a quarter of irrigated land suffers some degree of salinization, leading to lower harvests or, in the worst cases, complete crop failure. Salinization in some locations may be reversed by a process of flushing the salts from the soil, but this is expensive and time consuming. A more effective approach is to reduce the risks in the first instance by more careful water management and the use of more efficient irrigation techniques. Drip irrigation, for example, whereby the water is delivered close to the plant roots through a system of pipes, reduces water loss to less than ten percent. This compares to losses of between 40 and 90 percent through evaporation and drainage using more traditional methods.

SALINIZATION BY CONTINENT (% OF GLOBAL AREA AFFECTED)	
Africa	19.3
Asia	68.8
South America	2.7
North and Central America	3.0
Europe	5.0
Oceania	1.2

Source: The World's Water, 2000-2001

Water on a warmer planet

One of the big unknowns when considering future water use is the impact of climate change and global warming. The three warmest years since climate records began have all been recorded since 1998, and 19 of the 20 warmest years have occurred since 1980. There is already evidence that glaciers (one of the world's major stores of fresh water) are melting and lakes are beginning to dry up. In other parts of the world, too much rainfall has been a problem, causing flooding and destroying homes and crops. One of the biggest effects of global warming – the melting of the polar ice caps and the raising of global sea levels – could also have unforeseen impacts on the global water cycle.

Climate change is also set to put further pressure on existing freshwater supplies. There are warnings, for example, that a rise in sea levels could cause salt water to enter groundwater reserves and contaminate the freshwater supplies of over two billion people. Many of the world's largest coastal cities would be affected by such an event.

There are also worrying predictions that farmland in areas such as the Nile and Ganges deltas could disappear under rising seas. This would put greater pressure on water supplies as new areas of irrigated farmland are opened up to compensate for the loss.

In 2000–2001 and again in 2004–2005, Cape Town in South Africa was forced to introduce an emergency water savings programme as the reservoirs feeding the city began to dry up due to lower than normal winter rainfall. If we do nothing then it is likely that many of us around the world will face similar restrictions at some point in the future.

Part of the Perito Merino glacier in Patagonia, Argentina, falls into the ocean. The melting of glaciers is a sign of global warming – a major threat to future water supplies.

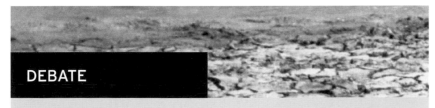

DEBATE

You are in charge

You are part of a team that has been asked by an environmental charity to help them design an environmental checklist for new water projects. With your colleagues, you must come up with three key points to go into the checklist and say why you have chosen them.

CHAPTER 4

Dangers to Health

Kai returns from the store empty-handed. He has some bad news: 'Mum, they've run out of water again!' His mother sighs in disbelief. Kai and his family have come to rely on bottled water from the superstore in recent years because their own supply has become contaminated with chemicals. They found out when Kai's younger sister became ill and the doctors told them to stop drinking the water from their tap. They don't know what has caused the contamination, but they suspect it might be from the industrial works on the other side of town, or maybe from the nearby farms that are always spraying their crops with chemicals. The local water company had said that by 2020 all the pollution problems would be cleared and the water would be safe to drink again, but five years on and despite their efforts, not all water supplies are safe and some have got worse!

What are you drinking?

Kai's story is a familiar one and there have been examples of water supplies contaminated by industrial and agricultural pollution harming people since the 1950s. In fact, unclean water is one of the biggest causes of death in the world and kills millions of people – especially young children – every year. At the start of the 21st century, one in five of the world's people lacked access to a regular, safe water supply and one in three lacked access to safe sanitation facilities. This latter statistic is of particular concern because human waste water and sewage is one of the worst pollutants in countries where sanitation facilities are poor or non-existent.

The problems relating to unclean water and sanitation are particularly severe in less developed countries (see panel), but water in richer countries can also be polluted. Industries, commercial farming, landfill sites and even households produce a daily cocktail of pollutants that find their way into the water system. These pollutants can include heavy metals, pesticides and medicinal drugs and have been linked to cancer, birth abnormalities and infertility in humans and animals. Many governments and water companies have introduced strict controls to try to filter out such pollutants, but some are very hard to detect and may be having long-term effects.

Some harmful substances may also be added naturally from geological sources. In Bangladesh, for example, naturally occurring arsenic is causing acute health problems in water supplies taken from groundwater (see pages 26–7).

Chemicals pour from an outlet pipe straight into a nearby water supply in Germany. For hundreds of years people have used rivers, lakes and oceans as dumping grounds for waste. This has left problems of widespread pollution today.

ACCESS TO CLEAN WATER AND SAFE SANITATION

Country/Region	Regular access to improved (safe) water source (%)	Regular access to improved (safe) sanitation facilities (%)
Brazil	87	76
China	75	40
Denmark	100	100
Ethiopia	24	12
India	84	28
Mexico	88	74
Nigeria	62	54
UK	100	100
USA	100	100
Less developed countries (average)	62	44
World (average)	82	61

Source: UN Human Development Report, 2004

Overloading the system

Historically, nature has often been relied upon to clean waste water and recycle it, through the water cycle, into clean, useable supplies. Wetlands, for example, perform a vital role in this respect, removing pollutants as the water passes slowly through them, like giant filters. However, many wetlands have now been built upon or drained for farmland, and this important function has been lost. In the USA, for example, around half of the Florida Everglades has been lost to urbanization and agriculture.

The earth beneath our feet also serves as a filter, the water slowly passing through layers of soil and rock, which remove some harmful compounds before the water reaches groundwater reserves. Today, many of the pollutants we produce are not able to be broken down or absorbed by the natural systems, and as we extract greater volumes of water for human use, the pollutants are increasingly contaminating our aquifers.

Groundwater pollution

As surface waters (rivers and lakes) have become more polluted, groundwater has been increasingly used as an alternative source of pure water. Scientists believed that groundwater would be free from harmful substances, but recent studies have shown this not to be the case. In some instances health problems have arisen from naturally occurring chemicals such as fluoride or arsenic. In Bangladesh for example, thousands of boreholes are contaminated with arsenic that occurs naturally in the underlying sediment. In Hajiganj thana of Chandpur district, in south-east Bangladesh, a survey revealed that 94 percent of the area's 12,000 wells contained arsenic that exceeded the safe

DAMAGE TO THE FLORIDA EVERGLADES ECOSYSTEM

- 50% reduction in area of the Everglades
- 90-95% decrease in wading bird populations
- 68 threatened or endangered species
- 2,467 million cubic metres of water lost from the system through discharge and unnatural seepage annually
- increased unnatural discharges of fresh water have damaged coastal estuaries
- the incidence of diseases affecting coral has increased tenfold since 1980
- 4,047 million square metres of the system subject to health warnings because of possible mercury contamination
- phosphorus contamination of Lake Okeechobee, the Everglades, and surrounding wetlands
- the rampant spread of invasive exotic species and the displacement of native species

Source: Living Waters: Conserving the source of life
(WWF, 2004)

level. If consumed, arsenic causes skin diseases, liver problems, damage to the nervous system and eventually cancer and death.

Fluoride is another naturally occurring chemical that has been found in groundwater in parts of India, China, Sri Lanka, Thailand and East Africa. Fluoride in small quantities is essential for good bones and teeth, but in excess it causes dental decay and damages bones and joints (skeletal fluorosis) to leave people in severe pain, or completely crippled. In China, over 1.6 million people may be suffering the effects of drinking water contaminated with fluoride, and in India estimates put the number at around 60 million. Children are particularly affected as their bones are still forming.

In addition to naturally occurring chemicals, artificial pollutants are now being found in groundwater across the world. Many of these pollutants are complex chemicals that are extremely dangerous to humans and wildlife. Underground petrol storage tanks at filling stations, for example, regularly leak petrochemicals into groundwater. These chemicals have been linked – even in quite small amounts – to an increased risk of cancer in humans.

This water supply in Khulna, Bangladesh, is a safe supply, known to be free from arsenic. Many water supplies in Bangladesh have been contaminated with arsenic that occurs naturally in the soils and rocks.

Pesticides, fertilizers, heavy metals, solvents and radioactive wastes have also been detected in groundwater reserves. Some of these chemicals were banned from use on the land many years ago because they are so toxic and are not easily broken down in the soils and aquifers. However, because of the slow flow rates and long storage times, they are only now showing in groundwater.

The worst is yet to come

This time-lag means that there is probably much worse to come. Chemicals banned as long ago as the 1970s are showing up in groundwater in the 2000s, and some banned since then may not show up for several decades. This means that by 2025 much of the world's groundwater could be facing serious pollution problems. To make matters worse, the newer generation of chemicals that may now be seeping into groundwater are much more potent than in the past. Agricultural pesticides in use now are up to 100 times more toxic than those used in 1975.

There are many new chemicals too, such as those used in the hi-tech computer and electronics industries, and some of these may have as-yet-unforeseen consequences. There is also little knowledge of what happens when various chemicals react and mix, as they might in the aquifers that meet our future water needs.

Nitrate pollution

One of the more obvious forms of water pollution is nitrate pollution. If you have ever seen a lake, stream, river, or even the

The spraying of fertilizers, pesticides and herbicides onto farmland is one of the world's major sources of water pollution. Rain carries the chemicals through the soils and into local water supplies.

sea, covered in a thick algae growth, then this is more than likely a result of nitrate pollution. Nitrates are contained within agricultural and domestic fertilizers, human and animal excreta, and leachate (liquid waste) from landfill sites. They accumulate in water systems in large quantities, feeding algae that form huge blankets known as 'algal blooms'. These cut off sunlight from aquatic plants and gradually starve the water of oxygen, leading to significant plant and fish deaths.

High nitrate levels have also been linked to a higher rate of miscarriage in women and to infant methaemoglobinemia, or 'blue baby syndrome'. Blue baby syndrome occurs when nitrates reduce the ability of the blood to carry oxygen, eventually causing suffocation and death. There have been over 3,000 known deaths as a result of blue baby syndrome since 1945.

CHEMICALS, CONTAMINANTS AND HUMAN HEALTH

Pollutant	Source	Effects
Arsenic	Naturally occurring in sediments and rocks	Skin diseases, liver problems, nervous complaints, cancer
Nitrates	Fertilizers, farm run-off, landfill sites, sewage	Blue baby syndrome, miscarriage, possible link to cancers
Fluoride	Naturally occurring in sediments and rocks	Dental problems, deformities and/or pains in bones and joints
Chlorinated solvents	Electronics, metals, plastics, textiles and aircraft factories	Links to reproductive disorders and some forms of cancer
Petrochemicals	Underground storage tanks	Several petrochemicals (e.g. benzene) can cause cancers even at low levels
Pesticides	Run-off from farms, golf courses, lawns; landfill or storage leaks	Possible link to infertility and reproductive disorders. Nervous system damage and cancers
Pharmaceutical /veterinary drugs	Pass into water system through human/animal urine and excreta	Possible impacts on fertility and reproductive function (especially from female contraceptive pill). Hormonal imbalances

Source: State of the World 2004 (Worldwatch Institute)

Cleaning our water

Ensuring access to water is only part of the challenge we face in the future. Making sure that water is also safe for drinking, or for watering our crops and animals, is just as important. In the UK some 110 million pounds (200 million US dollars) is spent each year removing pesticides from water, and in the USA an estimated one trillion US dollars will be needed between now and 2030 to clean up contaminated groundwater. A far cheaper option would be to reduce the pollutants entering the water system in the first place.

Reducing pollutants need not be expensive or complicated. Simple pit latrines, for example, are highly effective at reducing the volume of human waste entering water supplies, and boiling water before drinking or using it for cooking can kill almost all harmful bacteria.

Furthermore, there are simple farming methods that dramatically reduce the need for pesticides and fertilizers, 60 to 90 percent of which end up as waste in the environment. Mixing different crops (rather than growing a single crop in a monoculture) enables plants to better resist pests and diseases that could wipe out a single variety. Crops such as beans and peas (legumes) can also work as fertilizers as they have a natural ability to fix nitrogen in the soil. These methods have been used in

This scientist is taking samples of water near a waste outlet of a coal-fired power station in the UK. Careful monitoring can help to reduce pollution.

countries as diverse as China, Kenya, Cuba, the Netherlands, Indonesia and the USA. In nearly all cases the use of chemical inputs has fallen by around half while yields have remained the same or even increased.

Industries have also found ways to reduce the emission of water-borne pollutants, and landfill sites are now carefully monitored for their toxic leachate, which is siphoned off to prevent it entering nearby water supplies. In many countries, laws have been introduced to enforce such changes, but in other instances polluters have found that reducing chemical emissions not only benefits the environment but can also save them money.

Working with nature

By 2025, visitors to the Florida Everglades should again enjoy an area of outstanding scenic and wildlife importance. This is the ambition of the Comprehensive Everglades Restoration Plan, agreed in 2000. As well as the scenic and wildlife benefits of the plan, it also aims to boost water supplies in southern Florida and filter harmful wastes out of the region's water resources. After 50 years of neglect, the federal and state governments have realized that the best way to improve both the quantity and quality of water available to future generations is to work with nature. This is a lesson being repeated across the world as wetland ecosystems are finally acknowledged for their vital function in protecting wildlife and human wellbeing.

DEBATE

You are in charge
As the mayor of a small town, you are worried that the local water supply is highly polluted. You have an appointment with the central government to raise your concerns on behalf of the community. What issues will you focus on as a priority and why?

CHAPTER 5

Water Wars

It is 2025 and the fragile ceasefire between Indian and Pakistani forces over the waters of the Indus River is in danger of breaking down. Indian engineers were spotted in a gorge of the upper Indus yesterday and this has led to speculation that they are planning to build a dam. The dam would hold and divert the Indus waters to nearby farmland and further reduce the amount of water reaching already water-stressed Pakistan. Indian ministers claim it is just an investigation and there is nothing for the Pakistani authorities to worry about. Meanwhile, Egypt and Ethiopia are continuing to renegotiate their use of the Nile River following their war last year over Ethiopia's plans for a further dam and pipeline in the highlands. As a desert state, Egypt is entirely dependent on the Nile's waters, 84 percent of which originate in Ethiopia.

Looming conflicts?

These 'water wars' have not yet happened, but tensions over shared water sources are already very real. The United Nations has warned that water must be a priority issue in the early 21st century and that if nothing is done to resolve tensions there is an increasing likelihood of conflict. Sharing water resources need not lead to conflict, however, and there are good examples of sharing, such as the Great Lakes (shared by Canada and the USA) and the Rhine (shared by six European nations).

The scale of shared water resources is enormous. There are 263 international river basins (the area of land that feeds water into a primary river) in the world and between them they comprise almost half of the world's land area. In addition, 70 percent of the world's oceans are internationally shared, meaning that the majority of the world's water is a shared resource. The pattern for groundwater reserves is less well established, but many of these also span international boundaries.

A villager walks towards Bujagali Falls on the River Nile – one of many internationally shared rivers.

Who has the right?

The key question for shared resources is who has the right to that water. If a river rises in one country, for example, does that give that nation more rights than the other nations through which the river then flows? What is the situation when a river actually forms a border between two countries – who then has the rights to its water? These are difficult questions to answer and become even more so when the countries involved already face water shortages. Of the ten countries sharing the Nile waters, for example, several (Egypt, Sudan, Kenya, Uganda and Ethiopia) suffer periodic or long-term water shortages. Israel, Jordan and the Palestinian Territories, and India and Pakistan are other groups of countries that face water shortages and share a common resource.

SELECTED INTERNATIONAL RIVER BASINS

River Basin	Continent	Countries (in order of % share of basin within borders)
Amazon	South America	Brazil, Peru, Bolivia, Colombia, Ecuador, Venezuela, Guyana, Surinam
Congo	Africa	Congo DR, Central African Republic, Angola, Congo, Zambia, Tanzania, Cameroon, Burundi, Rwanda, Gabon, Malawi
Danube	Europe	Romania, Hungary, Serbia and Montenegro, Austria, Germany, Bulgaria, Slovakia, Bosnia-Herzegovina, Croatia, Ukraine, Czech Republic, Slovenia, Moldova, Switzerland, Italy, Poland, Albania
Ganges/Brahmaputra /Meghna	Asia	India, China, Nepal, Bangladesh, Bhutan, Myanmar
Indus	Asia	Pakistan, India, China, Afghanistan
Jordan	Asia	Jordan, Israel, Syria, West Bank*, Egypt, Golan Heights*, Lebanon (*disputed territory controlled by Israel)
Mekong	Asia	Laos, Thailand, China, Cambodia, Vietnam, Myanmar
Niger	Africa	Nigeria, Mali, Niger, Algeria, Guinea, Cameroon, Burkina Faso, Benin, Ivory Coast, Chad, Sierra Leone
Nile	Africa	Sudan, Ethiopia, Egypt, Uganda, Tanzania, Kenya, Congo DR, Rwanda, Burundi, Eritrea
Rhine	Europe	Germany, Switzerland, France, Netherlands, Belgium, Luxembourg, Austria, Liechtenstein, Italy
Tigris-Euphrates/ Shatt al Arab	Asia	Iraq, Turkey, Iran, Syria, Jordan, Saudi Arabia
Zambezi	Africa	Zambia, Angola, Zimbabwe, Mozambique, Malawi, Tanzania, Botswana, Namibia, Congo DR

Source: The World's Water, 2000-2001

Flashpoints

Between 1950 and 2001 there were just over 500 disputes over shared water resources. Most of these involved threats and angry exchanges and only 21 actually resulted in military action, 18 of which were between Israel and its neighbours. Nevertheless there remain numerous flashpoints around the world where water is a key issue. In several instances competition over water coincides with existing political tensions between nations. This is the case with India and Pakistan, which must share the waters of the Indus River, and with Israel and its neighbours, which share the Jordan River. In both cases these countries have gone to war several times in the last 50 years. Peace negotiations have today replaced conflict, but disagreements over the rights to shared water resources remain one of the main obstacles to a lasting peace in both regions.

Water ministers from India and Pakistan at a meeting in 2004 to discuss India's plans to build a new dam on a river shared by both India and Pakistan. The two countries have had several disagreements over the use of their shared water supplies.

In early 2005, Pakistan called in the World Bank to help resolve a dispute with India over India's plans to build the Baglihar hydropower dam on the Chenab River in Indian-controlled Kashmir. The Chenab feeds water into Pakistan's main agricultural region of Punjab and the Pakistani government is concerned that the dam will reduce the flow of water reaching the Punjab. Pakistan is also concerned that in the event of a conflict, India could use the dam to hold back or release water and cause serious drought or flooding in Pakistan. India says the dam will have no impact on the flow of water reaching Pakistan as it is only for generating electricity (HEP) and not for storage.

Working together

It is conflict over projects such as the Baglihar dam that could lead to future water wars. But the example of India and Pakistan also points to a way in which such wars can be averted.

The World Bank were called in to resolve the 2005 dispute between India and Pakistan because that organization had helped to create a treaty over the sharing of the Indus's waters (of which the Chenab is a part) in 1960.

Similar water treaties exist for other shared water resources, with at least 200 having been agreed since the 1950s. Some of these have taken up to 30 years to negotiate and are still subject to disagreements because conditions are constantly changing. The Nile Waters Agreement, for example, was signed in 1959, and the population and water needs of the nations involved have changed substantially since then. Egypt secured rights to the majority of the Nile's water during the initial agreements and even has the power to monitor the outflow of the Owen Falls Dam, located at the opposite end of the Nile in Uganda. Egypt now faces greater competition from the growing populations of the other countries that share the Nile. To avoid potential conflicts a Nile Basin Initiative was launched in 1999 in which countries work together to manage the river for the 300 million people who depend upon it.

Similar agreements are in place for the Danube in Europe and the Mekong in Asia. Such cooperation is essential if conflicts over water are to be minimized in the future. The UN and other agencies urge countries with shared water to use it as a unifying force and not a divisive one.

DEBATE

You are in charge
You are a minister in a country that has only a five percent share in a major international river. You desperately need to make more use of its waters in order to meet the needs of your people, but must convince the other three countries to allow you to use more water. What percentage will you ask for?

1. Increase from five to ten percent because the population has doubled since the last agreement was made.
2. Increase to 25 percent because all four countries sharing the river should have equal rights to the water.
3. Increase to 14 percent based on an equal share for each person living in the countries that share the river.

CHAPTER 6

Making the Most of it

It is 2025 and the town of Tremp in Spain has just been awarded a United Nations prize for water conservation. The story began in 2000 when the town suffered its fifth year of water shortages and decided something must be done. The community came together and developed a plan to make better use of the water they have. Rainwater is collected from roofs and stored for irrigating crops in the hot, dry summer. Waste water from bathing and kitchens is recycled through reed beds and then used to flush new low-flush toilets. Some houses have even installed compost toilets that use no water at all. An education programme has also helped everyone to reduce personal water consumption by up to half. Local businesses have developed new practices to reduce water use and prevent pollution of local water supplies. Since 2020 Tremp's water plans have been so successful that they are even selling surplus water to neighbouring towns.

Leaving a tap running is a simple waste of water that can easily be prevented through changing the behaviour of water consumers.

Taken for granted

It would be good news if all towns could be as successful as Tremp in making the most of water, but unfortunately most of us are very wasteful of water and pretty much take it for granted. Do you leave the tap on whilst brushing your teeth for example? If you do then you could be wasting over five litres of water every minute – the same as the daily minimum we are all recommended to drink.

Water is wasted in all manner of ways – in homes, in industries, on farms, in gardens and even by the water companies that supply us. It need not be like this and the changes needed are in many cases very small. Think about the toothbrush example again. If you and your family (assuming there are four of you) brushed your teeth twice a day for two minutes, but turned off the tap instead of letting it run, then your house alone would save 80 litres a day, 560 litres a week, and an incredible 29,200 litres per year. Now imagine everyone in your class at school (assuming 30 classmates) did the same in their homes. That would save an amazing 876,000 litres per year.

LEAKAGE AND LOSS OF TREATED WATER IN SELECTED COUNTRIES

Country	Percentage of treated water supply lost to leakages
Albania	up to 75
Czech Republic	20-30
Denmark	3
France	up to 50
Jordan	48
Singapore	5
Spain	24-34
Taiwan	25
USA	10-30

Source: State of the World 2004 (Worldwatch Institute)

The price of water

One way to reduce the amount of water that we use is to pay more for it in the first place. At the local store you may pay 55 pence (US$1) for a litre of bottled water (a lot more in many cases), but imagine if that were the cost of water coming from your tap. Flushing the toilet could cost you over £4 (US$7); a typical washing machine cycle would cost £33 (US$58); and a dishwasher load around £11 (US$19). As for watering the lawn, that could cost you over £500 (US$880) if you used a sprinkler for just one hour!

In reality of course we do not pay the same for water coming from the tap as we do for bottled water in the store. In fact in the UK the average price paid for both the supply and disposal (sewage) of a litre of water was around 0.15 pence (0.26 cents) in 2005 – over 360 times less than a bottled litre.

Perhaps this is part of the problem. We pay so little for the water we use that there is no incentive to save water. This is not true

Women collect water from a well in Zinder, Niger, in West Africa. Many women in Africa walk long distances several times a day to collect fresh water. When such labour is involved in obtaining water, people use it very carefully.

everywhere however. Many of the poorest communities in the world must purchase water at great expense. In Nairobi, Kenya, residents of the poorest slums pay around 20 times more for water from private vendors than wealthy residents pay for piped supplies from the Nairobi Water and Sewage Company. For the very poorest this can represent a substantial proportion of their daily budget. Elsewhere in Africa, Asia and other regions, people pay for water in the time and energy needed to collect it from remote sources. This burden most often falls upon women and children who may travel over five kilometres every day to collect water in a journey taking several hours.

As water becomes scarce, pricing it more realistically may be one of the only ways to make people realize what a precious resource it is. One way to do this is to install water meters in people's homes so that they pay for what they use. In the UK, water meters are now fitted to around a quarter of all homes and evidence shows that people consume less water when paying by meter than they do when paying a flat rate charge. Even so, the actual price paid is still very low. The problem is that water is considered by many people to be a basic human right (see Chapter 7) and so charging too much for water could prove deeply unpopular.

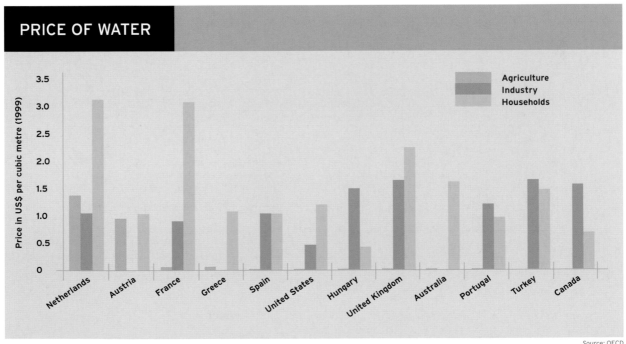

PRICE OF WATER

Legend: Agriculture, Industry, Households

y-axis: Price in US$ per cubic metre (1999)

Countries: Netherlands, Austria, France, Greece, Spain, United States, Hungary, United Kingdom, Australia, Portugal, Turkey, Canada

Source: OECD

Greater efficiency

Encouraging better use of the water we have could be one way of conserving supplies without having to put up the price of water. Improved water management in farming, for example, has been shown to reduce water use by over 50 percent. Though some of the technologies involved, such as drip irrigation (see page 22), can be expensive, others, such as improved timing of water applications, can be very cheap.

In the home, taking a five-minute shower instead of having a bath could reduce water use by over 80 percent. Fitting water-efficient washing machines and dishwashers could also allow reductions of 50 percent or more. Low-flush toilets can reduce the water needed for flushing by almost half. Special bags that hold around three litres of water can be placed in the toilet cistern to reduce the water held

A poster in Bhutan urges people to use water supplies carefully to prevent wastage. Education campaigns such as this are an important part of conserving water in areas with limited supplies.

and used for each flush. Leaks around the home should also be repaired. A tap dripping once every second for example, could waste up to four litres of water a day!

Water companies and governments can also do their bit to improve efficiency. In the USA, for example, up to 30 percent of the nation's water supply is lost through leakage, whilst in France it is as high as 50 percent. Where pipework is ageing, water companies face enormous costs to reduce leakages, but such waste seems wrong in a world where many people can barely get enough water to survive.

Consumer choices

The choices we make as consumers can also influence global water supplies. For example, our diets use far more water if they contain a high proportion of meat and processed foods. The average diet in North America or Western Europe requires around 5,000 litres of water per day. By comparison, the more vegetable-based diets of Africa and Asia require between 1,800 and 3,300 litres per day.

Buying water-efficient washing machines and dishwashers is another obvious way of reducing water usage. Many countries now have eco-labelling schemes to help consumers make such choices. Even the types of plants we choose for our gardens can help: if we opt for those able to tolerate drier conditions, we can reduce the need for watering.

DEBATE

You are in charge
Public education is considered essential in order to make people aware of the value of water and to help conserve future water supplies. You are responsible for a new water-efficiency programme. You must decide which three key messages you want to use in a national advertising campaign. What three messages would you choose and why?

CHAPTER 7

A Human Right for All

It is 2025 and Goreti has finally made it to the international court of human rights. She has come from northern Uganda and is taking the government to court because she says it is failing in its duty to provide her and her family with access to safe water – an internationally recognized human right. The Ugandan government says it cannot meet the new Convention on the Rights to Water that became law in 2015 because it is a poor country without the financial ability to pay for the necessary pipes and water treatment plants. Uganda is appealing for international aid to help it meet the needs of Goreti and thousands of others like her. Many countries are watching the Goreti case, because they too are finding it hard to provide water to meet the needs of their people, especially in those drier regions where there is a natural shortage of water. The outcome could influence whether the right to water is a reality or an empty statement.

A boy enjoys a fresh water supply in Samreboi, Ghana. Making access to water a right for everyone is a major challenge for the 21st century.

Water and human rights

At the start of the 21st century there is no specific convention on the rights to water, despite it being one of the most fundamental human needs. The right to water is contained within other agreements, however, such as the Convention on the Rights of the Child (1989) and the International Covenant on Economic, Social and Cultural Rights (1966).

The problem with these, say water campaigners, is that they do not give enough status to water and it is too often an assumed right in the same way as the air that we breathe. They argue that if water were made a very specific human right that could be agreed internationally then it would help to focus the minds of governments and oblige them to meet the basic needs of millions of the world's people. As it is, there are currently around 1.1 billion people who lack access to clean water; 2.4 billion without safe sanitation facilities; and two million who die each year as a result of water-related diseases – that is almost four people (most of them children) every minute.

MAKING WATER A RIGHT

A selection of statements from agreements that relate to the human right to water:

'... the human right to water entitles everyone to sufficient, safe, acceptable, physically accessible and affordable water for personal and domestic uses.'
General Comment 15 (2002), International Covenant on Economic, Social and Cultural Rights, 1966

'All peoples, whatever their stage of development and their social and economic conditions, have the right to have access to drinking water in quantities and of a quality equal to their basic needs.'
United Nations Water Conference, Mar del Plata, 1977

'Everyone has the right to have access to sufficient food and water.'
Section 27(1)(b) of the Bill of Rights, Constitution of South Africa, 1994

'In determining "vital human needs" special attention is to be paid to providing sufficient water to sustain human life, including both drinking water and water required for production of food in order to prevent starvation.'
Statement of Understanding accompanying the UN Convention on the Law of the Non-navigational Uses of International Watercourses, United Nations, 1997.

Meeting the rights

If a specific human right to water were to be introduced, many countries would find such a right hard to meet. Some parts of the world are already desperately short of water and the situation is deteriorating. Some of the organizations monitoring water supplies predict that 48 countries will suffer severe water shortages (struggling to meet even basic needs) by 2025 and that over half the world's population will lack access to clean water. In many cases, those with the worst shortages will also be some of the poorest countries. They will therefore face a double burden of not having sufficient water to meet the needs of the population, and great difficulty in funding any solutions.

International cooperation

A higher degree of international cooperation will be essential in order to avert a future water crisis and this cooperation could take many forms. Countries with common water resources must reach peaceful agreements on how best to share them. Countries with an abundance of water could also assist those with shortages through water transfers via pipelines or other methods. However, such transfers may bring with them a number of problems. For example, invasive plants or organisms may be transferred from one river basin to the other. Also, the loss of water from one basin may cause springs and wetlands to dry up and upset people's way of life.

Other forms of cooperation could also have a dramatic impact.

A freshly laid lawn is watered in Sixth October City, Egypt. Many believe water should not be used for such luxuries.

Cancelling the debts of some of the world's poorest nations could free up valuable money to be spent on meeting basic water needs. Sharing experience in water-saving technology and practices could also provide great benefits. Israel, for example, has developed world expertise in drip irrigation and is using this in – amongst other places – the Rift Valley of Kenya to help flower and vegetable growers make the most efficient use of a scarce water supply. Countries can also work together to ensure the environmental protection of water resources by agreeing international standards and pollution controls.

Taking responsibility

Ultimately, you and I as individuals can also play a role in avoiding a future water crisis. The choices we make in our everyday lives can have a remarkable impact and as we learn about the value of water we should make it our responsibility to share that experience with others. Caring for water becomes even more important if you live in or visit a country that is particularly short of water. Many popular holiday destinations suffer extreme water shortages and yet are expected to use valuable supplies to fill swimming pools or water golf courses. Learning to respect water for the invaluable commodity that it is would be a good lesson for us all to learn.

What if we do nothing? When it comes to water, doing nothing is not an option.

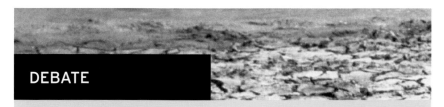

DEBATE

You are in charge
The United Nations has put forward a new motion that there should be a universal human right of access to safe water for drinking and adequate water supplies to meet other basic needs. You are a minister in a country with severe water shortages and where many people do not yet have access to safe water. Will you support or object to the motion? What are your reasons?

Glossary

aquifer An area of porous rock, sand or gravel that stores water underground, sometimes for millions of years. Humans have drilled wells into aquifers to use this store of water.

arsenic A naturally occurring chemical that is poisonous to humans.

atmospheric water vapour Moisture in the earth's atmosphere that includes clouds, mist and fog.

blue baby syndrome A common name for a medical condition called methaemoglobinemia that deprives the blood of oxygen and has been linked to high levels of nitrates in drinking water. It makes the skin appear blue in colour.

borehole A deep hole dug or drilled to reach water stored beneath the ground.

brackish Salty – normally describing a mixture of fresh water and seawater.

chlorinated solvent A solvent (glue) in which chlorine is a major ingredient.

climate change The process by which long-term climatic patterns are observed to vary from the expected norm. Climate change in recent times has been linked to global warming.

contamination The act of making something unclean or polluted, such as when chemicals are poured into a water supply.

convention An agreement, normally at the international level, between different groups of people or different countries.

desalination The process of removing the salt from saline water in order to produce fresh water that is suitable for human consumption.

drip irrigation A highly efficient form of irrigation that uses tubing and computers to deliver precise amounts of water directly to the roots of the crop.

eco-labelling A system of labelling products according to their environmental impact, such as how efficient they are at using energy or water.

ecosystem The contents of an environment, including all the plants and animals that live there. This could be a garden pond, a forest or the whole Earth.

erosion The removal of soil or rock by the forces of wind, waves, ice and rain.

fertilizer A chemical mixture (often nitrogen or phosphorus based) used to add fertility to the soil in order to promote plant growth.

fluoride A chemical compound of fluorine that is used as the active ingredient in many toothpastes.

glacier A large mass of compacted ice and snow that contains vast quantities of fresh water.

global warming The gradual warming of the Earth's atmosphere as a result of carbon dioxide emissions and other greenhouse gases trapping heat.

groundwater Water that is present within porous rocks, sands and gravels underground.

heavy metal A family of metals, including lead, mercury, copper and cadmium, that have a particularly heavy density. They are often toxic.

HEP Electricity generated by water as it passes through turbines. These normally require large dams across river valleys that form artificial lakes behind them.

hydrological Of or relating to water.

infiltration The process by which water passes through a porous material such as soil, sand, gravel or rock.

irrigation The artificial application of water to crops.

leachate A liquid formed when water enters a landfill site and carries diluted chemicals and metals with it as it passes through the rubbish.

low-flush toilet A toilet that reduces the amount of water needed for a flush.

monoculture The cultivation of a single crop species.

particulate air pollution Air pollution caused by small particles in the air, such as dust.

permafrost An underlying layer of rock and/or soil that remains permanently frozen throughout the year.

pesticide A chemical used to combat pests that destroy crops.

petrochemicals Any one of a family of chemicals created from crude oil.

pharmaceutical Relating to the manufacture or sale of medicinal drugs.

pit latrine A simple toilet consisting of a covered hole (pit) in which human waste collects.

pollutant Something that contaminates or pollutes the air, soil or water.

radioactive waste Waste material from radioactive processes and facilities. It can include radioactive material itself and substances that have been in contact with radioactive material.

run-off Water that runs across the surface of the land to enter the natural water system. Run-off is associated with over-application of water in agriculture and often includes diluted fertilizers and pesticides.

saline Having a high salt content.

salinization A process in which salts become highly concentrated in water or soils, affecting plant growth and even causing land to be abandoned.

sanitation The provision of hygienic toilet and washing conditions to prevent the spread of diseases associated with human waste.

sediment Particles of material that are normally carried suspended in solution (in water) before settling to the bottom of a river or other body of water.

solvent A form of glue that is normally made of toxic chemical compounds.

sustainability Development that meets the needs of today without compromising the ability of future generations to meet their needs.

tube well *See* borehole

water vendor An individual who sells water to customers.

wetland A land habitat in which the presence of water for all or most of the year is a dominant feature.

World Bank A global organization that makes loans available to governments for large development projects such as new dams for supplying water.

Further Information

Websites

www.evergladesplan.org/index.cfm
The site of the Comprehensive Everglades Restoration Plan for the Florida Everglades, with information about the history of the Everglades, the threats it faces and the plan to restore this important wetland and its environmental functions.

news.bbc.co.uk/hi/english/static/in_depth/world/2000/world_water_crisis/default.stm
A BBC website report on the world water crisis, with information and links to topical news articles and examples from around the world.

www.righttowater.org.uk
A site devoted to the campaign for making water a fundamental human right. Information on the history of the rights to water, how you could get involved and up-to-date news on progress.

www.wateraid.org/
An international NGO that works with many of the world's poorest communities to secure them basic water supplies and sanitation facilities. Their site contains fascinating insights, useful case studies and tells you how you could help.

Books

21st Century Debates: Water Supply by Rob Bowden (Hodder Wayland, 2002)

Earth Strikes Back: Water by Arthur Haswell (Belitha Press, 2000)

Earth Watch: Water For All by Sally Morgan (Franklin Watts, 2000)

Looking At Energy: Water Power by Polly Goodman (Hodder Wayland, 2005)

Debate Panel answers

Page 9:
There is no single answer to preventing a future water crisis. It will require a combination of different measures by governments, businesses and individuals.

Page 15:
Cost and sustainability are two of the most important considerations. In areas where water resources are shared, the security of a supply is also important. With good international agreements, the transfer of water is a good option.

Page 23:
Your checklist could include the following checks:
1. To what extent does the project disrupt the natural water cycle? (This could affect downstream users and the environment.)
2. Are the benefits to people greater than the losses that might be suffered by those affected by the project? (Sometimes projects may not benefit many people.)
3. Has the project been designed with the long-term future in mind? Is it sustainable? (Some water projects may have long-term effects that should be carefully measured.)
4. Have alternatives been properly researched and considered? (Sometimes there are better alternatives to the project under consideration.)

Page 31:
You might want to focus on what national regulations there are to control and monitor the quality of water. Are there laws that can be used to help clean up water supplies if they are found to be polluted? If pollution comes from beyond the city boundaries what will the government do about the source of the pollution?

Page 35:
The division of internationally shared water resources is very difficult and there are no certain answers. Countries sharing water resources must reach a compromise based on their needs and on the availability of alternatives.

Page 41:
There are many different messages you could choose. They might include:
1. Recognize the importance of water to life on earth.
2. Recognize how little of the world's water is available to humans.
3. Consider the real costs of water.
4. Understand the importance of shared responsibility for a common good.
5. Save water today for tomorrow's needs.

Page 45:
It is a difficult position to be in, but water is so important to life that it should become a right for all people. You should support the motion and seek the assistance of the international community to help you meet the targets of the new rights.

Index

Page numbers in **bold** refer to illustrations.